.

Money, Wealth & Freedom

A Little Book of Working Wisdom

Steve Straus

First Edition: September 2013
Printed in the United States of America
Light on the Water Press
Pottsboro, Texas
ISBN: 978-09721747-3-2

Published in partnership with Suncoast Digital Press, Inc.
Sarasota, Florida

To Thomas J. Leonard.

Without him, none of this material
would have been created.

"Most of what makes a book 'good'

is that we are reading it at the right moment for us."

—*Alain de Botton*

Contents

Foreword xiii

Introduction..1

Money.   Wealth.   Freedom. 3

Value 9

Opportunity 10

Self-Worth 11

Allow-Receive-Have 12

Freedom vs. Liberty..13

Real Goal vs. Tool Goal 14

Emotions 15

The Need To Be Self-Regulating..16

Free From Self Pre-occupation..17

Freedom Provides Security 18

Self-Awareness...19

Adult?...20

To Not Know..21

Under-promise vs. Overpromise 22

Self-Deception 23

Life Purpose...24

Your Sources of Energy 25

Be Aware vs. Beware 26

It Is What It Is..27

Quick Response 28

Self-reliant vs. Responsible 29

Freedom to be a Human 30

Contentment vs. Happiness 31

Escape Key..32

Obstacles 33

Luxurious vs. Luxury 34

Freedom 35

SPENDING MONEY TO GET APPROVAL...36

FREEDOM VS. SECURITY..37

TOLERATING STRUGGLE..38

DESIRE VS. NEED 39

JOY VS. RELIEF...40

ADDING VALUE VS. CUTTING COSTS...41

CHOICE VS. SACRIFICE 42

A NEW RESOLUTION ON NEW YEAR'S RESOLUTIONS..................43

ADMIRE VS. ENVY...44

CHECKBOOKS 45

MORE AND LESS...46

WEALTHY VS. MATERIALISTIC 47

FLOW VS. HOLD 48

IMPORTANT VS. PERSONAL 49

BUSINESS—GOOD VS. NO VS. BAD...50

JOY OF DEATH..51

BEING FOUND OUT 52

WHAT NEEDS TO GET FUNDED? VS. WHAT DO I NEED TO PAY FOR?........53

FINANCIAL SUCCESS IS A REQUIREMENT, NOT A NICETY...........54

ATTACHMENT...55

TOLERANCE VS. TOLERATION 56

WHAT'S NEXT? VS. RETIREMENT 57

INTEGRITY..58

SEVERAL VIEWS OF FREEDOM 59

RESOLVE VS. FIX...60

MONEY 61

SCARCITY 62

INVESTIGATION 63

FREEDOM ALWAYS HAS A COST 64

YOU ARE 65

CREATIVITY VS. CREATIVE REPACKAGING......................................66

LIBERTY AND SECURITY...67

FREE 68

IN THE PROCESS VS. ATTACHED TO THE OUTCOME 69

Flow 70

Doing Well..71

Freedom-To vs. Freedom-From 72

Making A Difference..73

There Is No Should In Giving...74

Abundance...75

It Never Hurts to Ask...76

Index..77

Facilitator's Guide..83

Facilitator Questions 85

Acknowledgments 87

About the Author...89

FOREWORD

By Debbie Mrazek

In my thirty-two years in sales, I have done millions in sales and I have also helped a lot of other people create millions in sales. So I was thrilled when *Steve's 3-Minute Coaching* (S3MC) began years ago as a weekly jolt to the brain to help us think about, consider, look at and question different things each week. The act of doing this was like what they taught us in high school Physics class—for every action there is an equal and opposite reaction—the weekly dose of S3MC—which, yes, really only took 3 minutes or less—was a catalyst to step out of your own thinking (and yet deepen your own thinking) about yourself or things that you were doing to get to success. And, what success these little bits of wisdom have created for me and others in the past eighteen years!

My colleague, mentor, and dear friend, Steve Straus, is like most of us. He did not have a career that was mapped out and charted from birth. His journey has taken him to some places he planned to go and others he could have never dreamed. Along the way he has gathered the money, wealth and freedom that he (no different than the rest of us) strived for. But, also he accrued incredible wisdom. His spirit of giving back, as well as wanting to grow his business and continue to attract new clients, led him to share his wisdom.

When Steve told me he was going to write a book and take his years of ideas, thoughts, distinctions, and thought-provoking questions and put them in one place, I was thrilled to think of how many more people will now experience his gifts and be able to transform them into things— sometimes miracles—that they could never have thought of or created with just their own thoughts.

In the world we live in today there is a lot of information, ideas and thoughts out there to choose from. This book is the real deal in that its intent is not to just push information out there but to help people see beyond themselves and their day-to-day life to be able to create a life that is TRULY them, and which can end up being more than they could have ever imagined by themselves.

Money, Wealth and Freedom is made up of Steve's words but Steve's words come from not just studying topics, but actually studying people, working with people, sharing experiences and living life; his writing is never just theoretical but has impact which helps others create, dream, imagine and accomplish more than they ever dreamed possible.

Lucky for you, this book allows you to have years of his wisdom at your fingertips versus just getting a little piece each week! It allows you to have this phenomenal coach to carry with you every day like you carry the keys in your pocket….imagine this being another key that helps to get you where you want to go.

Through three different businesses of mine, Steve has been my coach, and each week I have had a shot of his wisdom with *S3MC*. He has been my Yoda, training and coaching me and my business through each level to insure growth. I have always felt that he cared about what I was doing and was vested in helping with growth, ongoing success and our legacy. Steve's wisdom you will find in this book is like an insurance policy for the economy—you are covered when the economy is good or bad for money, wealth and freedom.

By reading and practicing what you learn in this book, you will have the same opportunity that I've had, and my friends and colleagues have had, and many others worldwide that I don't know have had to transform their thoughts, their businesses, and their lives. You will discover you have more potential in you than you ever imagined, and that you now have a powerful resource right at hand to help you achieve the greatness that to this point you might have only dreamed.

Debbie Mrazek, President, The Sales Company
Author, *Field Guide to Sales: The All-Weather All-Terrain Guide to Selling*

Money, Wealth & Freedom

Introduction

You are not alone. Many people struggle with money, wealth, or freedom.

> *Needlessly so.*

Did you grow up with enough teaching and guidance around the topic of money to give you the tools and confidence you need to enjoy a wealthy lifestyle?

> *Few people have had good guides or any guidance, ever.*

Do you often have money come in, but the next thing you know, it's disappeared?

> *Knowing you can stop that hero/zero cycle and accumulate whatever you want is one of the most freeing things you can learn in this lifetime.*

Do you envy others who live a wealthy lifestyle—envying not just their money but their sense of calm and strength?

> *It's possible for you, too.*

Do you sometimes suspect that your issues around money, wealth or freedom spring from your own deep inner programming?

> *Awareness can be yours. New perspectives bring freedom.*

Money. Wealth. Freedom.

These three words get the attention of most people. We all want more of each of them.

Most people seem to think that by getting *more money* the other two will fall in line.

Not true! This book will not only show you how to have all three, but will also help you make changes **which will cause them to show up in your life**.

What is this book? It's distinct from a "how-to-get-rich" book, some magical treasure map to untold riches. Those never work. Instead, we are here bringing clarity and new perspective to many of the core issues which contribute to being stuck in a less-than- satisfying state. When those core issues are exposed and dealt with— often quite easily, sometimes merely with the flash of an "ah-ha!"—the outer, more tangible, metrics of more money, more wealth, and more freedom show up.

New perspectives, distinctions, and understanding inform and cause new thinking, actions, and results. Your new results become sustainable because those deep changes automatically drive your new, more pleasing results.

Most of the material in this book is original; some is gleaned wisdom from my personal experience, from mentors and coaches, and from my highly successful coaching clients; and some is universal wisdom, the gems you already have a deep knowing about which my words, examples, and questions can bring to the surface. The really good news here is that while this book has useful information, its prime purpose is to evoke the wisdom which already lives within you.

What are Money and Wealth and Freedom?

Do you believe it is possible for you to have more of each? You are correct- it is. But first let's clear up a common misconception.

Money and **Wealth**, while related, are two different things.

Money is money—income, cash, coin of the realm, revenue, bank balances—money is known by many names. Attracting money, receiving it, and having and using it are pretty simple activities. From your first job you began to understand money and what it could do for you.

Having more money in this life is useful. You have come into a world in which money is as essential as water, air, and food. Some people think it unseemly to acknowledge that, but it is true. You must have a reasonable amount of money to have any kind of a decent life.

Part of this book is focused on money, what it really is, having more of it, and using it in ways which improve your life. A key purpose of this book is to help you identify your own inner barriers—blocks—about money. You then may find you can release the thoughts, conscious or unconscious, which block you from *having and enjoying all the money you want*.

Next is Wealth. Wealth includes money, but is so much more. Wealth includes how you *feel*, not just what you *have*.

Wealth shows up in many forms—money, of course—and even more importantly, what having that money does for you. For some, more money adds tension and burden. For others, it reduces tension and burden. What each person thinks and believes about wealth determines how they feel about it.

The key to the **Wealth** component of this book is to help you get clear on just what wealth means to you, defining it, clarifying your thoughts, and resolving your obstacles to being as wealthy as you want. Then the money part of wealth will flow to you much easier. But with your expanded sense of wealth, you will end up with far more than just the money.

Money and Wealth lead to Freedom. Freedom is a part of our wiring as humans. It is at the level of your DNA; each and every cell of your body is designed to be free to live its full purpose. Everyone has a built- in desire to be free. The technical term for this is the desire to be "self- regulating," meaning that you want to be able to determine what's next for you, *without restriction.*

While the strongest souls can choose Freedom under even the most dire circumstances, such as POWs, the sense of Freedom discussed in this book is most similar to what one has when one has *reserves —* freedom to choose.

Freedom is a big deal and directly relates to money and wealth. Some would say that freedom is the only reason to have money and wealth. Think about that. Is there any better result of having more money and wealth than to experience more freedom? Built into every action is the desire and/or expectation that the action will cause you to feel better. What better "feel better" is there than feeling free?

What is the history of these gems of wisdom?

The genesis of *Steve's 3-Minute Coaching* (S3MC) was for a weekly business networking group of which I was a member. It was a leading- edge group brimming with strong, successful members. I wanted to add value to them, and being fairly new to the group, offered to create and deliver a short, unique bit of thought and inspiration from the then-still- emerging profession of Coaching. (It also gave me guaranteed weekly visibility with the group!)

Soon they asked me to fax each week's offering, using the then-high-tech fax broadcasting from my PC. (It *was* mid-1995.) They might have to miss a meeting, but wanted to not miss the S3MC. Faxing turned into early AOL email and then to today's automated distribution systems and social networking tools.

There currently are subscribers on six continents. It used to go to all seven due to a single subscriber at McMurdo Station in Antarctica, but she rotated out.

It has also been translated into French and redistributed by a Coach in France, and into Spanish and redistributed by a Coach in Madrid, Spain. I'm grateful to them both for increasing access to this material.

Okay, that's the back story on this book. I had a desire to add value, wanted visibility, responded to readers' requests to upgrade the delivery medium, and wrote something every week—900+ issues so far. In retrospect, it seems pretty easy. All can be found on www.Steves3MinuteCoaching.com.

I wonder what wonderful thing you could produce, writing just once a week? I'd love to hear about it.

How to get the most out of this book to deepen and expand your experience.

At your innermost, private, unique Self, you are always benefitting from bits of wisdom. They evoke the "ah-ha's" which cause a shift in how you see yourself and your journey. A change in perspective can change what you see, hear and feel. I remember the first time it dawned on me that I was the latest version of a source lost in history. As the lyrics of a song describe, "Blood flows from back and back and back, like a river from a secret source." That change in perspective changed how I see the present moment. Or at least it provided the opportunity for that change; it was up to me to see it. Wisdom operates like that. Somewhere in this book are perspective-changers for you, individually and personally.

On another scale this book may be a source of thought and discussion for you to share with your family—the people closest to you, whether by birth or by choice. Most people find their life journey is richer when shared. When you can bring to the people who are most meaningful in your life some thoughts, ideas, language, yes, even some wisdom, it not only serves them, the process of sharing evokes additional insight for you. There are families who use this material as discussion points to foster communication, understanding, connection, and growth among the members. While some families literally read and discuss the topics at dinner once a week, or enhance goal-setting or planning sessions by using favorite principles, others simply enjoy spontaneous referencing which is useful and possible when everyone has read the material.

And then, given the universal nature of the topics of Money, Wealth, and Freedom, you may be like others who use the information in this book to set the tone for a business meeting. Reading/sharing one appropriate entry from the book at the start of a networking group, a meeting of the sales staff at your company, or a strategic planning session of your favorite not-for-profit organization, can be an important few minutes of focus to catalyze the effectiveness of the meeting. Organizations have been doing this for years.

My intention is that you find one or several ways to have this material be useful for you personally. I have received comments and testimonials from fans of this material all over the world who report the positive impact of reading and applying these principles, distinctions and other gems of wisdom. What do I want for you? I want for you to mine the richness of this little book to find and receive what you most want. To help you do that I've included several resources.

In addition to the traditional table of contents, there are two other access points within the Index in the back of the book. First, there is a list of the entries grouped by major subject. This means if you are interested in looking at each entry which relates to the major subject of Money, you can do so directly using this list. The other major subjects are Wealth, Freedom, Purpose, and Awareness. Of course, many of the entries pertain to more than one major subject, thus are included in each appropriate list.

The second access point is the "S" number which precedes the title of each entry in the index. This is simply a unique number which was assigned to each entry the day it was originally published in the *Steve's 3-Minute Coaching* blog. When referencing a particular entry, many people find it easier to remember a short number than the specific words in the entry's title. (The eBook versions of this book, such as for Kindle, have all the index listings internally linked to corresponding S3MCs for instant reader access.) Finally, there is a resource for the use of this book by study groups. It is a list of thought-provoking questions for you or another group facilitator to use to foster a discussion. Of course each entry has, as a part of it, a "Coaching Point" which is a question pertaining to that entry.

The general questions in the Facilitator's Guide are to augment those coaching point questions. Obviously you may also create other facilitation questions of your own. I would love to hear those from you.

This **Money, Wealth** and **Freedom** book is designed to assist you in increasing and having more money (a very practical level), defining and having more of all the kinds of wealth you desire (an expanded level), and experiencing your personal, unique definition of freedom (a much higher level of life).

This book is not designed to tell you what you *should* have. It is designed to help you discover and define and move into the life you most want, **your** life.

VALUE

CATEGORY: Principle

Lie # 1: Time Is Money.
No, it isn't. Have you ever put in a lot of time and received little (or no) money? And have you ever spent just a little time and received a disproportionately large amount of money? You probably answered "yes" to both questions. In spite of the evidence, many people still believe that if they just put in more time, the money they want will come. But time and money are unrelated, unless you think they are. You may want to re-think.

Lie #2: Work Equals Money.
No, it doesn't. In the above, substitute "work" for "time." If work equaled money, you would be surrounded by wealthy people. It may be that you have worked enough to have a lot of money. Do you?

The Truth: Value Equals Money.
We have lost the truth of this because we no longer trade chickens for corn. When we did, we were very clear about a "chicken's worth" of corn. We understood the value of what it took to grow the chicken and the corn. We were trading for value. When we perceived the value of what we were to receive was worth the value of what we gave up, a deal was struck. Money is just a convenient form of chickens/corn, but it has allowed us to forget the basic principle of delivering and receiving value. It's not about time or work; it's about value.

Coaching Point: *Ask yourself each morning, "How can I add value today?"*

Opportunity

CATEGORY: Principle

Opportunities abound. At least they do for the person who is looking and aware. The more you look for opportunities the more you see. But few people spend much of their time looking. They are content to just take whatever shows up.

To have an opportunity is one thing, to take advantage of it is another. Taking advantage means you get into action. You do something about it, you don't just observe. A highly successful mentor, from many years ago, taught me to leave white space on my calendar. In other words, don't schedule every minute of my day. He said that many opportunities have a short window and having the time and space to respond quickly was one of the attributes of his success.

And taking advantage of an opportunity is not the same as taking advantage of someone. Just because you are looking for opportunities, and you see one, and you look around and notice that no one else is seeing it, and you then act on it, is not the same as cheating/putting something over on/taking advantage of someone. If your day is spent looking for ways to take advantage of someone (of course no one reading this!), then you will not have the space to look for opportunities.

Coaching Point: *Your world has abundant opportunities. What kind are you looking for?*

SELF-WORTH

CATEGORY: Quote

"Often our self-worth
is tied up in our net-worth."
—*Steve Straus*

Coaching Point: *Do you know that you are not your money?*

Allow-Receive-Have

CATEGORY: Principle

If you're not having the life you desire, you may want to see if you're stuck at any of these three junctures.

ALLOWING. At a conscious level you say you desire something, but at an unconscious level you list all the reasons why you can't have it, as in (consciously) "I want to be financially wealthy," (and unconsciously) "but then people will only want to be around me to get my money." To fully allow you may have to look at and let go of some of your assumptions and old beliefs.

Allowing is making sure the door is open.

RECEIVING. When receiving something you've not had, it must feel a little (or a lot) unusual, uncomfortable, un-normal. Of course it does, it's new! For example, "Wow, this great new relationship is moving really fast. I'm feeling a little overwhelmed by my emotions." To be an effective receiver you may have to practice enjoying the inflow.

Receiving is letting what you want come in the door.

HAVING. Many people don't have the capacity or permission to enjoy what they have received, as in "How can I have so much when others have so little?" You may feel you have to earn something before you can have it. To have a high *havingness* level you may need to resolve some self-worth issues.

Having is keeping and enjoying what has come in the door.

Coaching Point: *Does any part of you resist this? Which part?*

Freedom vs. Liberty

CATEGORY: Distinction

Most people are at liberty to go where they want and do what they want. Sometimes we take our liberty for granted. This point was demonstrated a few years ago when a visitor to our home from the then-USSR was amazed to learn that we could decide, at any time, to fill the car with gas and head out to a city across the country without asking for permission or needing "travel papers." Liberty is external; it is something granted to you from the outside, such as bylaws and regulations.

Freedom comes from the inside. You are controlled by your beliefs, standards, values and self-perceptions. If these internal factors say that you cannot do something or be someone, then you are not free, even though you have liberty. Freedom lives inside liberty.

Freedom requires liberty, but being free to choose comes from you.

Coaching Point: *What keeps you from being free to choose?*

REAL GOAL VS. TOOL GOAL

CATEGORY: Distinction

Goals can be useful. The issue is whether your goals are real or merely tools.

A Tool Goal is one which will get you to an outcome that you believe will then set you up to get your Real Goal. In other words, it's a tool, not the real goal. With a Tool Goal, instead of going directly for what you really want you make it harder by working obliquely.

"I'd never do that," you might say. Really? Do you have any money goals? Do you think you need to first get the money to then get what you really want? That would be a Tool Goal. Why not go for the Real Goal and let the money — or whatever it takes to get the real goal — show up?

By the way, a Tool Goal is not the same as an incremental goal. An incremental goal can be a reasonable step along the path to your Real Goal, such as a plan to lose five pounds next month to get to your ultimate weight goal in one year. The difference is you know that an incremental goal is only a step in the right direction.

Most of us have been taught to work, effort, and struggle to get what we want. To someone with that built-in belief, working toward a Tool Goal seems normal. Unfortunately, it also has the effect of limiting options on how the goal must be realized.

A Real Goal is a definition of what you want to Be, Do, or Have. It is the payoff. For real.

Coaching Point: *What keeps you from going for what you really want?*

EMOTIONS

CATEGORY: Principle

We are only as effective as our emotions allow us to be. It is, therefore, vitally important to be aware of your emotions, to resolve any which are not useful, and to use the rest to your best advantage.

That's a tall order. Most people are merely passengers, riding on the backs of their runaway emotions. What can you do to change?

First, acknowledge the control your emotions have over you. Most people can't do this because they are either blind to their truth or it's too scary to admit. Until you can acknowledge the control your emotions have, they win.

Second, know that even though an emotion has controlled you up to now, you can become free of the grip of it. You are fortunate to live in a time when a wide array of easily affordable processes and technologies are available to assist you in loosening its grip.

Finally, decide to, and take, action. Get help. Find methods which work for you and begin resolving your issues one by one. Make a game of it. In a relatively short time you'll start noticing new degrees of freedom and increased energy.

When you do, you will become much more effective.

Coaching Point: *What is one situation where you know you are controlled by an emotion?*

THE NEED TO BE SELF-REGULATING

CATEGORY: Personal Needs

This is a common need. To be self-regulating means to be in control of your own destiny. It means you get to determine how your day will unfold. No one else decides what your actions should be. In numerous job satisfaction surveys, the need to be self-regulating has ranked at the top — higher than increased pay.

Picture the stages of development to adulthood — from small child to youth to teenager to adult. The wise parent allows their child more and more self-directed action as they grow through each stage. (Not an easy thing for a parent to do, but that's another subject!) As the child demonstrates mastery they are given more freedom.

Then the magical day arrives and the young adult thinks they are free... free at last! Then they go off to college or to work for a company and quickly learn that someone else is still determining their limits. Many find they are not free. Not self-regulating.

If you see yourself in the above situation, why? What keeps you from being self-regulating? Security? Inertia? Not enough pain yet? Do you think it's impossible to be self-regulating?

It's not impossible, but first you have to want it to happen. Awareness is the key to filling this need, the need to be self-regulating.

Coaching Point: *The desire for freedom/self-regulation is even deeper than a need. Do you know it's part of your deepest human wiring?*

FREE FROM SELF PRE-OCCUPATION

CATEGORY: Quote

"Real Freedom is being free from self pre-occupation."
—*Don Beck*

Coaching Point: *How many people do you know who are almost totally focused on themselves? Are they fun to be around?*

To know what you want and go for it is, of course, useful, but if you exclude others due to your Self pre-occupation, you slow down your progress.

Most people want to feel free to fully express their life. The traditional message is, "Don't be egotistical, selfish, or self-centered."

A more powerful life model is to give yourself a gift, the gift of real freedom, by including others in your journey. Check how you're doing by counting the number of people you actively support and who support you.

When you let go of your Self pre-occupation, you will be free. Who helps you feel the most You?

Freedom Provides Security

CATEGORY: Principle

Everyone has a built-in need for security, but just because you do doesn't mean that maintaining security has to be the focus of your life.

Instead, to focus on freedom means that you are creating a life of choice; freedom to choose who you are with, what you do, and where you go. If you decide to make creating freedom your focus, what do you do next?

It is hard to be free if you're dragging around a lot of "stuff." Clean up your physical environments. Handle the incomplete relationship issues from your past. Identify the things you are tolerating and resolve them. This look backwards, and the resulting work, may take up to a year. Get help. It doesn't have to be hard.

Next, build reserves in all areas of your life — reserves of money (of course, everybody goes there first), but also reserves of energy, love, opportunities, resources and knowledge. Having reserves, abundant reserves, means never *having* to do something. Instead it means only doing what you choose to do. Being at choice is what freedom is about.

Freedom is a responsibility. If you choose to be free, you are also choosing to be responsible for creating and maintaining it for life. You will not have anyone else to blame for your lack of freedom.

But once you've made the leap, you will no longer worry about security.

Coaching Point: *This isn't what you were taught when you were growing up, is it?*

SELF-AWARENESS

CATEGORY: Principle

Have you ever noticed that people who know Who They Really Are have a self-assuredness about them? They carry themselves with a natural ease and comfort. They are fully engaged in life, yet have no attachment to forcing their point of view on others. And they are not easily sucked into confrontation.

This can be somewhat disconcerting because they don't play the game like everyone else. The person who knows Who They Really Are is playing a different game. It's the most important one — their own.

This does not mean they are alone—far from it. Most people like this know that involving others in their game is useful and appropriate. The outcomes they are heading towards touch many. They are not being selfish; they're contributing to others because that is part of their game.

Coaching Point: *Who do you know that knows Who They Really Are? What have they learned that allows them this freedom and focus? What of it can you put in place?*

ADULT?

CATEGORY: Great Questions

"What is the most adult thing I can do for me, now?"

Coaching Point: *Does the question sound selfish? It could. The key is "adult" — past ego, past childish, past should.*

Look at your goals, what you want, what you desire. Look at your resources — time, money, people, ideas.

Be conscious. Be aware. Be bold. Only then, choose to act. Or not.

If you do this adult thing, what outcome do you want from it?

To Not Know

CATEGORY: Principle

It's easy to get wrapped up in trying to figure everything out. Your mind is a wonderful thing. Thinking, planning, and discerning are all useful tools, but they become hindrances when overdone. Life is unimaginably complex and constantly striving to understand it is exhausting.

Trying to always Understand is one of life's traps.

One of the greatest freedoms is the freedom to Not Know. When you let go of needing to know, wonderful, magical things can appear. You return to the wonder and delight you had when you were first discovering your world as a child.

When trying to Understand, life is a constant puzzle filled with traps. Fear, uncertainty, and doubt abound.

When you have given yourself permission to Not Know, life shows itself to be extraordinary and miraculous and you enjoy a level of expansion which transcends your mind.

Coaching Point: *Where are you already comfortable Not Knowing and where else can you expand on it?*

UNDER-PROMISE VS. OVERPROMISE

CATEGORY: Distinction

When you under-promise it means you are promising to do less than you know you can do. It's a good habit and you get a sense of relief or comfort from the reserve it creates — reserve that allows you to easily over-deliver.

Frequently overpromising comes from a desire for approval, or from a fear of losing a piece of business, or because we like (and need) the adrenaline rush associated with living life on the edge. It is this friction that is unhealthy, yet it is how many of us deliver results — at a high personal cost.

It may take a number of opportunities for you to consistently learn to under-promise. Start with small, unimportant (i.e. non-life-threatening!) occasions such as when you promise to send a letter (add a day), or when you promise to meet someone (add 15 minutes). As you start to experience the sense of calm strength which accompanies the reserves you are creating you will naturally grow to under-promise (and then automatically over-deliver) in all areas of your life. Enjoy the freedom!

Coaching Point: *What is a core driver which compels you to over- promise? Afraid they won't like you? Might not hire you? Won't include you?*

Self-Deception

CATEGORY: Principle

Goethe said, "Oh, how sweet it is to hear one's own convictions from another's lips." And, "We are never deceived; we deceive ourselves."

People in the public eye are reminded to never read their own press releases. And you, for sure, should never read your own resume — it's written to make you sound like you've been the right hand of God! Press releases and resumes can be slippery slopes to self-deception.

Self-awareness comes from being willing and able to look at your current truth.

Where are you stuck? What makes you feel yucky? Of what are you afraid? Are you, solely, responsible for the outcomes in your life, or do you believe your life is the result of what has happened to you?

When you look inward at your truth you will begin to see what needs to be healed/resolved/let go of/re-framed. When you've started to handle that deep conditioning and resolved it, you can see clearly what your life is about.

Only by becoming self-aware can you deal with that which you have let deceive you.

Coaching Point: *Self-deception feels warm and familiar, self-awareness feels (at first) uncomfortable. Are you willing to be a little uncomfortable in order to experience freedom from self-deception?*

LIFE PURPOSE

CATEGORY: Quote

"A Life Purpose is not a job description,
nor is a job description a Life Purpose.
They are related, however."
—*Scott Ochoa*

Coaching Point: So often people get caught up in their job/occupation/ profession/business that they forget to pause and ask, "Now, what is my Life about?"

Earning a living. Making money. Working. Trying to keep the wolf from the door. These labels of various activities tend to result in a job description. Job descriptions are useful tools to help you focus your energy, measure progress, and provide structure for your efforts. So, for sure, create any useful job description you want.

But keep in mind the well-known quote from Socrates: "The unexamined life is not worth living."

Before writing your next job description, take some time to examine your Life. What is really important to you? What is less important than that? And even less than that? And then not really important to you at all? What do you value? What legacy do you want to leave? In other words, who are you, really?

Get help with this if you find solo self-examination daunting.

Coaching Point: *Look through these Life lenses to review your current job description. Are they in sync? Can they be?*

YOUR SOURCES OF ENERGY

CATEGORY: Principle

Do you know what your sources of energy are? Meaning, whatever it takes for you to have enough energy to make it through the day.

Some possibilities are: adrenaline, shame, fear, victimhood, unmet Needs, proving something, competition and winning. Others are: your business, your position in the community, and that old favorite, money, or more likely, the lack of it. These all provide energy and all of them are expensive.

"But I've got to make a living," you say. Fine. Make your bucks, but don't look to that as a source of energy. You could just choose to live more simply.

It's all about the choices you make as to what your energy sources are and will be.

Try some of these: reserves, peace, happiness, love, service and life. All are healthy sources of energy, but you may not have thought of them that way. You need plenty of energy every day. Just choose to get it from healthier sources.

Coaching Point: *What is one new source of clean, healthy energy you can easily start developing right now?*

BE AWARE VS. BEWARE

CATEGORY: Distinction

"Beware!" is the sign outside a dangerous area. It is an indicator that you may be at risk, and it's certainly useful to know where risk and danger are present. But spending too much time looking for risks diverts time from looking at what's great about your present.

Awareness is one of life's great leverage points.
• The more aware you are, the more options you see.
• The more options you see, the more choices you have.
• The person with the most choices has a clear advantage.

How do you use your awareness? Focusing too much of your attention on possible danger limits your choices. People with limited choices have limited responses available.

Be aware of your surroundings. Beware of what's potentially dangerous. Just don't let your aware-ness be consumed by your beware-ness.

Coaching Point: *Do you experience the freedom of awareness?*

It Is What It Is

CATEGORY: Principle

Typically, when you say "It is what it is" you feel either up or down, either gratitude or resignation. This is interesting because the statement has no inherent meaning. It has only the meaning you give it.

"It is what it is" can be a liberating place from which to operate— always aware, always open to see clearly, always open to respond to the truth of what is so right now. This is a place of strength for you because you're neither judging nor interpreting.

However, how many times have you heard people use the phrase and accompany it with a sigh? Kind of victim-y, "it's beyond my control," no choice in the matter, being at the effect of the situation.

When you regularly respond to "It is what it is" without making up a story, you'll feel a strong sense of freedom.

Coaching Point: *What do you need to change in order for you to feel gratitude that "It is what it is?"*

Quick Response

CATEGORY: Quote

"You must seize the opportunity of a lifetime
during the lifetime of the opportunity."
—*Author unknown*

Coaching Point: *Do you have the reserves of time and money to act quickly when an opportunity presents itself?*

SELF-RELIANT VS. RESPONSIBLE

CATEGORY: Distinction

It's considered a mark of maturity and wisdom when you assume responsibility for your life. Responsibility means you realize it is largely up to you for how your life turns out. You are not a victim, living as a result of someone else's whims. You have a measure of freedom.

Being self-reliant is a step up from being responsible. When you are self-reliant, you not only take care of what happens (being responsible), you also take care of things which might happen. You become a good planner. You build reserves. You have alternatives.

For instance, a responsible person might have a strong home insurance policy. A self-reliant person will also have financial reserves to take care of events not covered by the policy.

A self-reliant person has even more freedom than someone who is merely responsible because he or she has planned for contingencies.

Coaching Point: *Neither Responsible nor Self-reliant are shoulds. They are want-to's. Do you want to be Self-reliant?*

FREEDOM TO BE A HUMAN

CATEGORY: Quote

"People who live in the post-totalitarian system know only too well that the question of whether one or several political parties are in power, and how these parties define and label themselves, is of far less importance than the question of whether or not it is possible to live like a human being."
— Vaclav Havel — Last President of Czechoslovakia; and First President of the Czech Republic.

Coaching Point: *Freedom has many descriptors. What does it mean for you to "live like a human being"?*

Contentment vs. Happiness

CATEGORY: Distinction

When asked what they want most people say they want to be happy. When asked what would make them happy, they trot out a list of external conditions — more money, time, love, experiences. However, after they receive the things that make them happy, the happiness fades, and they end up with the dreaded "more" disease, on the hunt again.

Happiness is about externals. It is transient. It can be adrenaline-based. It can even be addictive. It is a useful intermediate step in your development, but it is not a useful destination.

To be content is to be satisfied with who you are, not wanting to be more than you are or to be anyone else. Contentment is sustainable and has a calmness, peace and strength associated with it. It is based on an internal frame of reference.

However, to be content does not mean that you quit learning and growing. You simply cease striving and start living. And the living you do will be a reflection of who you are, not because you're trying to be happy.

Coaching Point: *Have you experienced the difference in the feeling of contentment versus happiness?*

Escape Key

CATEGORY: Great Questions

"What is the Escape Key which returns me to my Main Menu?"

Coaching Point: *Occasionally in life we get caught in dead-ends, scary places, confusion, and doubt about what to do next. Most modern software and "smart" devices have an Escape Key function.*

Your Main Menu is the place from which you know how to navigate. It's a place of comfort and certainty, a Reset point from which you can begin again.

What are your Escape Keys (you probably have more than one) in the areas of spirit, relationships, business, health, contribution, learning, and wealth?

OBSTACLES

CATEGORY: Principle

Recently re-reading the entire collection of Calvin and Hobbes cartoons, written and drawn by Bill Watterson, I was struck by a recurring theme of Calvin's and how it shows up in adults, too.

Calvin, a six-year-old kid, and Hobbes, his stuffed tiger/best friend/confidant/co-conspirator, experience life through their limited lens since not much wisdom can be gathered in six years. As a result he/they are continually bumping into obstacles to having what they want and are, each time, amazed at their outcome.

The behavior they repeat is excessive self-referencing. Now, if you are a reader of my blog and emails (S3MC), you know I'm a fan of self-awareness, of knowing who you are and what your life is about, and then expressing it fully. Therein lies contentment, joy, contribution, and growth.

But Calvin — and we — can fail to see what is really so. He chooses to ignore physical laws (i.e. gravity), the appropriateness of parental responsibilities (such as mentoring), the two-way nature of healthy relationships (poor Susie), and the big one, his belief that he already knows everything and whatever shows up to the contrary is wrong!

We laugh at Calvin's exploits, oblivious when we behave similarly. Are the obstacles really outside us and we're merely at their effect? Or is our lack of awareness the real obstacle?

Coaching Point: *If you are repeatedly not getting what you want, what are you not seeing?*

Luxurious vs. Luxury

CATEGORY: Distinction

These two words look similar but are dramatically different, similar to the difference between having a satisfying life vs. having an impressive life-style. The key to this distinction is in what is felt. To feel luxurious is to experience your life from an internal frame of reference. There's something deeply satisfying and authentic — authentic to you, from you, and about you. You can enjoy the feeling of luxuriousness, and you know it does not define you. It is a by-product of the expression of your life journey, not the definition of it. Your luxurious life can be comprised of a surprisingly few number of things or many; it doesn't matter.

Luxury, on the other hand, slips into an external frame of reference where you can begin to define yourself by what you have and what others can see. (My friend, Willie the Barber said, of a guy he knew, "He may not have much, but what he has, you'll see it.")

A focus on accumulating luxury can lead to playing a role, trying to be seen as *somebody*. And if surrounding yourself with luxury is an attempt to get over feeling needy, you will always feel uncomfortable because you know, at a deep level, it could all disappear in a moment. "It," that luxury thing, is not who you really are.

Enjoy accumulating and surrounding yourself with fine things, experiences, travel, simplicity, relationships, whatever feels satisfying and luxurious to you. Enjoy it. Expand it. Even share it, if you want. Just know that you are far more than the items of luxury which may be involved.

Coaching Point: *Doesn't the unfettered word "luxurious" feel really good?*

FREEDOM

CATEGORY: Quote

"Ultimately we know deeply that
the other side of every fear
is freedom."
—*Marilyn Ferguson*

Coaching Point: *What would happen if you started to focus on the freedom instead of the fear?*

Spending Money To Get Approval

CATEGORY: Quote

"The point is that we are constantly trying to win people's approval because we are not taught to grant ourselves our own approval. In doing so, we usually spend a lot of cash frantically buying things and giving money away, hoping that somehow these actions will make us okay.

Either people accept you or they don't. You did not come here to be manipulated, just to keep people happy. What you are is what you are. You can change it. But first you have to accept it, for it is the truth. In accepting yourself, you don't have to get into a huge ego trip, but you do have to come to the point of being satisfied with what you are.

Once you can accept yourself and feel comfortable with that, then the world accepts you   It is only when you feel insecure about who you are that other people don't like you. Have you ever wondered why? Because basically, people who don't accept themselves are very insecure. That insecurity is projected, others react negatively. It reminds them of their own vulnerability."
— *Stuart Wilde*

Coaching Point: *It's not easy accepting yourself — warts and all — but it is necessary in order to change your spending patterns. Who can help you?*

Freedom vs. Security

CATEGORY: Distinction

Do you want to retire with freedom or with security? Both, you might say.

If you were to poll people about their definition of "financial independence" you would find most describe it in terms of freedom — freedom to travel, read, play sports, spend time with friends and family, and similar notions. That's what most people would say.

But most people would be lying. Oh, not lying in the sense that they're telling you a falsehood, but lying in that they are not conscious of their real reason for accumulating financial reserves — which is security.

Security is a pain-avoidance process. "If I have enough money, I won't have to worry about where my next meal/house payment/ medical expense payment/etc. is coming from." Having enough money means avoiding painful consequences.

Freedom, on the other hand, is a joy-maximizing process. Freedom to choose, freedom to go/not go, freedom to express your life in the fullest terms you can imagine, these are all ways to experience joy.

Freedom has risk. Security seeks to minimize risk. Freedom wants to expand your life. Security is willing to restrict. Freedom builds roads. Security builds walls.

If you are working to provide freedom for yourself but what you really want is security, then realize you are working at cross-purposes. Put your energy into what you really want, either freedom or security, and watch how much easier life gets.

Coaching Point: *I'll bet that once you get security handled you'll go for freedom, so why not go ahead and focus on freedom now?*

TOLERATING STRUGGLE

CATEGORY: Principle

Have you ever noticed how some people seem to struggle in life? Struggle with money. Relationships. Health. Some struggle with discovering the purpose for their life.

This may sound harsh, but struggle is a choice. Oh, maybe not a conscious choice; some may have bought into struggle through early conditioning or through some unfortunate later incident. And, yes, some have even made a conscious choice to struggle to justify living as a victim.

However they got there, know this — you don't have to struggle. If you are struggling right now, you don't have to continue. Get help; it's tough to get out of struggle alone.

Coaching point: *What is the payoff for you to tolerate struggle? Can you any longer afford the cost of that payoff?*

Desire vs. Need

CATEGORY: Distinction

True desire is quite different from a lot of other things which get (mistakenly) called desire. Desire is a natural and useful part of the human condition. Nothing has ever been created in this world without first being an emotion-based thought, a desire.

The confusion around desire is mostly because desire is not about pain. You and I will do more to avoid or minimize pain than we will to maximize pleasure. Desire is about pleasure.

Needs — and wants, wishes, requirements, shoulds — are about pain. There is the sense that something is "off," "missing," "wrong," or "ill," and must be fixed before you can be whole. Needs can masquerade as desires. Needs can override desires.

Here's a check list to determine which is in play:

Desire pulls. Needs drive. Desire guides. Needs just want away from. Desire is from your inner-most being. Needs are from your egoic mind.
Desire is soft and encouraging. Needs are loud and demanding.

The shortest path to discovering your true desires, and living them, is to get your needs met. Handle your past. Clean up your fears. Get help resolving your barriers.

As that noisy, painful stuff diminishes, your desires will become obvious. They will serve as your guide to living the life you came here to live.

Coaching Point: *What true desire have you been ignoring?*

Joy vs. Relief

CATEGORY: Distinction

When you feel the difference between these two conditions a major tool for having a great life will be in your grasp.

Take a moment and feel what it was like the last time you felt joy. Was it related to an event, a child, an accomplishment, an awareness, a freedom? What was true for you the last time you felt joy? As you recall this event, what does it feel like in your body? What is your breathing? Your facial expression? What's possible? Other feelings may be associated with joy such as freedom, contentment, eagerness, energy and fulfillment.

Next, pause a moment and recall a time when you recently felt relief. Had you just handled something that had been bothering you? Do something about that which you had been procrastinating, something you had been dreading? Did a pain stop? As you recall this relief event, what does it feel like in your body? Your breathing? Your tension?

When you feel joy, you are energized, enlarged, made whole, filled — you inhale.

When you feel relief you exhale, let go, feel drained, you have escaped.

Joy comes when you live your values, who you really are, your core beliefs. Relief is when you temporarily fill a need and stop discomfort. Joy pulls you forward, it's a *toward* energy. Relief is when you have escaped from something, an *away-from* energy. The more you resolve your needs, the more free you are to live your values and feel joy.

Coaching Point: *Is it okay for you to feel joy? A lot?*

ADDING VALUE VS. CUTTING COSTS

CATEGORY: Distinction

When the going gets tough in business, most folks automatically think of how they can cut costs in order to survive. There's another way to go.

Remember a time when you, either as a consumer in a retail transaction or as a business person dealing with one of your vendors, were pleased by receiving more value than you planned on. Those occurrences may have been rare, but notice that the ones you remember feel really good. Of course they do; everybody likes to receive added value.

So why not think of how you can cause those feelings in your customers by creating ways to add value to them? When they experience and feel that, you have set yourself apart from the automatic-cost-cutting horde. Besides, cost cutting only leads to a race to the bottom where nobody wins.

Often, adding value costs no money, only some of your time and your intention to add value. Because you want to do business that way, this is no real cost at all.

Coaching Point: *This Distinction is, of course, applicable to business, but can you think of ways you could add value to the meaningful relationships of your life?*

CHOICE VS. SACRIFICE

CATEGORY: Distinction

A political leader of an emerging country was asked about the great sacrifices she had made during her country's rocky road to freedom. She responded that she "had never sacrificed, merely made choices."

Her distinction is an interesting one. Most people seem to buy into the belief that they make sacrifices from time to time for a cause, a loved one, a job or a principle. They seem to like, or at least are comfortable with, the idea of sacrificing.

The truth is all you do is make choices — about what you will do or not do, about what you will support or defend. Your choices determine your direction, and to some extent, your outcomes.

If one of the outcomes you want is to feel that you have sacrificed, then realize that is only a choice you make.

Coaching Point: *Are you "shoulding on yourself" or are you at choice?*

A New Resolution On New Year's Resolutions

CATEGORY: Principle

At the start of a year it's popular (not very effective, but nonetheless popular) to write a set of New Year's Resolutions. In them we list all the negative traits about ourselves which we want to change and we resolve to change them.

Much more effective is to list all your core values:

• What do you stand for?

• Who are you really?

• What brings you the greatest sense of satisfaction?

• How do you spend your time?

• Where do you spend your money?

Answering questions like these will quickly show you what you value; not what you think you should value, but what you really do. When you know your core values, you can start to allocate more of the new year's time and resources to enhance your life, rather than trying to fix what's wrong.

Coaching Point: *What do you really, really value?*

ADMIRE VS. ENVY

CATEGORY: Distinction

It is a fine line that separates these, but a chasm in the difference.

When you envy someone there is a feeling of lack on your part; you want what they have. This can lead to resentment, even malice.

To admire is to enjoy someone's attributes or situation. This may manifest as pleasure or even wonder.

Which did you feel — admiration or envy — the last time a coworker landed a big sale or got a promotion or got praised? The interesting thing about this is that it's not about them at all. It's about you. What is lacking in your life that keeps you from being able to admire others' successes or fine attributes, without feeling envy? Your answer will lead you to the next thing you can strengthen in yourself.

The result will be freedom.

Coaching Point: *Doesn't admiration feel really freeing to you?*

CHECKBOOKS

CATEGORY: Quote

"There are few problems which can't be beat to death with a checkbook. Just don't attract problems which are bigger than your checkbook."
— *Steve Straus*

Coaching Point: Of course, having problems at all is a waste of your time and energy, but until you learn to transcend having problems (yes, you will!) practice looking at a problem and first asking, "How can this be resolved by a little money?" Most people are reluctant to take this approach for two reasons.

One, they've been taught to not spend money if it's a problem they can fix personally. However, if doing so is not your highest and best use, don't do it; hire someone for whom it is their highest and best use. It frees up your time and gives them a chance to shine.

Second, people say they don't have the money. What they mean is they are unwilling to reallocate funds from other uses, say pleasure activities. Remember, getting free of problems is pleasurable.

So, put your attention on why you're here, what your life purpose is, and what the next thing for you to do is. In other words, the big stuff. Let your checkbook handle the small stuff.

Coaching Point: *What is a current problem you can deal with using your checkbook?*

More And Less

CATEGORY: Quote

"People rarely have more than they will not allow themselves to have less than."
—*John Barnes*

Coaching Point: *Most people get enough (money, for instance, or it could be love, time, peace, etc.) to avoid having something unpleasant happen. When they get enough (the amount "they will not allow themselves to have less than"), they stop. What if you focused, instead, on having all you want?*

Wealthy vs. Materialistic

CATEGORY: Distinction

While lots of people want to be wealthy, there are also many who feel something is wrong with it.

When you are materialistic you find meaning in "stuff." It's a way to feel good about yourself. Your attention is on the "it" which you have.

Wealth is a different state of mind. When you are wealthy you may have many things, but your focus is on who you are and the life you are here to lead. The stuff you accumulate is merely a part of your journey. You may enjoy it. You may be glad you have it. But you are not defined by it. Your meaning comes from a deeper place.

Coaching Point: *Can you afford to be wealthy?*

Flow vs. Hold

CATEGORY: Distinction

This is a distinction which can require a major shift in your approach to life because most of us have been trained our whole lives that, in order to have a comfortable life, it is good, and even necessary, to gather as many possessions as possible — money, cars, homes, toys. We then naturally slip into the mode of protecting and defending them, using energy to hold onto them.

This holding energy is energy that cannot be used to enjoy life, to grow yourself, expand relationships or discover your true gifts. Holding is fear-based and a reflection of your ego.

To create yourself as a part of the flow is an alternate way of approaching life that frees up all of your energy to truly live *your* life, not an inherited or imposed one. When you shift to put yourself in the flow you'll find that people, money, opportunities and situations come to you rather than you having to chase after them. Instead of being egobased you become Self-based.

An interesting result of shifting to flow is that you will probably find yourself with more money, more love, toys and experiences than before, but you won't have the attachment to them you did!

Coaching Point: *Isn't Flow easy?*

Important vs. Personal

CATEGORY: Distinction

Are there important things you need to do or have done? And do you ever take it personally? Most people answer "yes" to both questions because they've got them collapsed together. Pulling them apart will clarify things for you.

First, whatever you do, do it well. Treat it as if it's important. Because it is. Doing things shoddily or in a half-hearted way is inviting unsatisfying results. To be aware, with focused attention, while doing complete work, is a recipe used by most highly successful people.

Taking things personally is another matter because you pay an emotional price. That's because, at some level, you are defining yourself by external markers. When those markers get met, you're able to feel good for a bit. When not met, you feel not so good. If you think you have to take something personally in order to be able to treat it as important, then something else is going on.

There is a wonderful freedom and strength that comes from the emotional detachment of being able to treat everything as important without having it "mean" anything about who you are.

Coaching Point: *What is one thing which used to be personal but is now (merely!) important?*

Business—Good vs. No vs. Bad

CATEGORY: Distinction

[Yes, this is a rare triple-header Distinction.]

To attract good business is obviously better than having no business at all. But the key to this distinction is in the *no business* versus *bad business* end.

Bad business is business which costs you more than it gives you. The costs may show up as money, time, energy, or emotions. You know what bad business is—it's the business you regret having gotten. It's the customer you wish you could fire. It's the client telephone call you dread making (or receiving). Bad business diverts your attention and energy from serving your good business.

The problem is, you don't recognize bad business before you take it on. All potential business can look like good business, if you squint your eyes enough!

An easy way to recognize the potential of new business is to see if it fits the definition of your ideal client profile. If it does, it will probably become good business. If it doesn't, learn to turn it down. Having no business is better than having bad business.

Coaching Point: *Do you have a list of the attributes of your ideal client?*

Joy Of Death

CATEGORY: Principle

The Joy of Death!? What? How can there be joy in death?

Sure, you know intellectually you're going to die, but most people tend to try to ignore the fact. Put off thinking about it. Hope it never happens.

By doing so they lose a valuable resource. Death gives you a framework. It gives you the edges.

When you embrace the truth of the certain death of your physical body — irrespective of your religious or spiritual beliefs — you embrace the full arena in which you now live. You include the edges and within the edges is freedom—to create, to express, to live.

Like a frame helps define a painting, the space to create your life is enhanced by enjoying your awareness of death.

Coaching Point: *The certainty of death sets you free to get after your life, doesn't it? With joy?*

Being Found Out

CATEGORY: Great Fears

The Fear of Being Found Out is about believing you have something to hide. Believing you have deficiencies. The possible shame you could experience. It's about "what would they think?"

Notice the pattern. This whole fear is from your inner dialogue, stories you made up—or were made up for you. (Perhaps to control you, shame, shame, shame.)

The questions to ask yourself, then, are: "What do I fear about being found out?" (Quantify it. Name it.) and, "What can I do about it?" (Clean something up? Let something go? Heal something? Finish something? Start something?)

The Fear of Being Found Out is simply a call to action. When you find yourself surrendering to this fear use the feeling as an indicator, like you would a blinking light on the dashboard of your car warning, "Low oil pressure!" When you fear being found out, instead of running from it, take an action.

Living with this fear is way too expensive. And you'll probably find out most of what you fear exists only in your imagination, *they* really don't care!

Coaching Point: *Or maybe you DO have some skeletons-in-the-closet you're not proud of. Pick one and handle it. Whatever the emotional cost, what might the payoff be for you? Freedom from fearing being found out?*

WHAT NEEDS TO GET FUNDED? VS. WHAT DO I NEED TO PAY FOR?

CATEGORY: Distinction

Instead of assuming you need to pay for something, consider these funding alternatives:

• Get a strategic partner and share the costs

• Get an equity investor (their money, your "sweat equity")

• Get a project investor (retain your ownership; share the profits)

• Use a crowdfunding Internet site

• Ask to pay for it only after you've added your value and sold it

• Ask for a volume discount even on the first unit you buy

• Ask for extended payment terms

• Sell it first (get paid in advance), then buy it or build it

Coaching Point: *Do you see that the list of funding alternatives is endless? Who can help you get creative with this?*

Financial Success Is A Requirement, Not a Nicety

CATEGORY: Principle

The 7 Keys to Financial Success (adapted from Thomas J. Leonard)

1. Be profitable today rather than assuming you'll be profitable soon due to increased income/sales. It also means that you create/save extra everything all during your day — extra time, extra opportunity, adding extra value, extra cash, extra investment, extra knowledge, extra awareness.

2. Expect a 20:1 rate of return on cash or time invested in your own personal or money-making projects. Using this measure will help you take yourself more seriously. It's a great filter.

3. Leverage (but don't put yourself at excessive risk) what you already have. We all have plenty of something, whether it's cash, time, intellect, ideas, connections, or experience. Leverage it.

4. Put yourself in the Flow (a progressive, healthy and profitable community). Where there is Flow, there is money and success.

5. Handle your blocks around money. Having blocks is completely predictable, normal, expected and fixable.

6. Be on a financial path. This means that you are consistently saving, increasing income, learning how to convert ideas into profit centers, etc.

7. Come from a desire to serve people and feel fine about making a profit. Shift from being a helper, contributor, assistance center, to being someone who offers what they have at a price that is worth paying for.

Coaching Point: *You don't need to do all of these at once. Which one is the easiest for you to start on, right now?*

ATTACHMENT

CATEGORY: Principle

High on the list of human conditions which keep us from having the life we really want is the condition of being attached to things. Attachment occurs when we really need for something to be a certain way in order to feel Okay. This need will rear its head and cause us to do things which we might not otherwise do, all because we want to feel Okay, or good, about ourselves. Therefore, being attached to an outcome is ultimately a loss of freedom.

Attachments can take many forms. Attachment can be mistaken for passion, beliefs or desires. You can tell the difference by checking how you feel. If you can still feel Okay about yourself when something is not the way you want it, even when you passionately want it, then you are probably not attached.

You are not your hair, your watch, or your car. You are not your marriage or your professional title. And don't let your net worth get tied up with your self-worth.

If you ever suspect (or have been told) that you have an attachment, the best corrective technique is to go to the extreme to release it. When you do, you will both validate the existence of the attachment and set the stage for its quick healing. Trying to talk your way into gently dropping the attachment is like trying to slowly remove an adhesive bandage. Quick and dramatic is better.

Coaching Point: *Do you believe it's possible to live free from having any attachments?*

TOLERANCE VS. TOLERATION

CATEGORY: Distinction

A toleration is something that is an irritant, a nuisance, or perhaps even painful. It's something that causes you to spend energy just by carrying it around, even when you don't do anything about it. In fact if you did do something about it, you would stop wasting the energy.

Areas in which you may have tolerations are your body (shape or weight), your money (not enough or too hard to get), your relationships (unsatisfying or even damaging), your environment (messy desk or broken appliance), and your freedom (what's that?). The fact is, we humans are easily capable of carrying around many tolerations, at great personal cost.

To exhibit tolerance is to see that things are the way they are for a reason and relax into reality. You can't change the world. You can't change someone else. You can only change how you react.

Tolerance is the skill of bending with the world so you can direct your energy to create what you want. Tolerance gives you energy. To suffer tolerations costs you energy. Notice the difference.

Learn where it's useful to rise to tolerance and where it's useful to handle a toleration and stop the pain.

Coaching Point: *Have you noticed how peaceful — and, surprisingly, powerful — it feels to experience tolerance?*

WHAT'S NEXT? VS. RETIREMENT

CATEGORY: Distinction

For a long time the life model has been: work to accumulate assets, then retire and, hopefully, live off the assets. It's the model which served our parents and their parents. In retirement one is supposed to relax and enjoy oneself, in part as a reward for having worked long and hard.

In recent decades a different model has emerged. It calls for viewing work as more than a process to accumulate assets. In this model your work is a source of enjoyment and satisfaction, not just money, because the work you choose is an expression of your life purpose.

As they approach the end of their current work, more and more people are looking for What's Next? rather than Retirement. Some are especially good at answering the What's Next? question because they have practiced by changing careers several times.

Coaching Point: *What's Next for you?*

INTEGRITY

CATEGORY: Principle

There are three energies that you use to create your experience of life — your thoughts, your words, and your actions. If you are not experiencing what you want to experience, it is probably because what you are thinking, saying and doing are not the same things. In Coaching language, you are thus out of integrity.

"I sure do want to lose 10 pounds" as you have a second dessert is an out-of-integrity situation.

"I'm a loving man of God" as you vote to exclude *those* kind of people from your environment is an out-of-integrity situation.

Believing that there is something "wrong" with being rich while working to accumulate money is an out-of-integrity situation.

As a bonus, when what you think, speak and do are the same, you feel a powerful peacefulness.

Coaching Point: *Do you notice how good integrity feels?*

Several Views Of Freedom

CATEGORY: Quote

"Everything that is really great and inspiring is created by the individual who can labor in freedom." —*Albert Einstein*

"Freedom is an internal achievement rather than an external adjustment." —*Adam Clayton Powell, Jr.*

"Uncertainty is the fertile ground of pure creativity and freedom.

Uncertainty means stepping into the unknown in every moment of your existence." —*Deepak Chopra*

"The whole world is a door of liberation, but people are unwilling to enter it." —*Hui-wu*

Coaching Point: *Where is your door to freedom?*

"I'm going to Fiji!" said Truman Burbank.

Resolve vs. Fix

CATEGORY: Distinction

Most people seem to enjoy fixing things. Something is broken, fix it. Something is out of whack, fix it. It can be very satisfying to fix stuff. So satisfying that some people look for things which need fixing because they get their "fix" from fixing! For them, their ability to fix things is part of their self-identity. Without a problem to fix, they can feel somewhat adrift.

A fix can be (and frequently is) temporary because you're usually fixing a symptom of a deeper problem.

To resolve something is generally permanent because you're getting to the source of the real issue.

For instance, sales are down, so you can fix that by making more calls. Or, resolve the problem of reduced sales by studying and discovering that a fundamental shift has occurred in your market and you will benefit by repositioning your offering to be in alignment with the new market realities.

Another example of resolve versus fix is with emotional stuff. You can learn to live with a negative emotion — fix how you react to it — or resolve the underlying issue and never have it recur again.

Fixing can be like playing the whack-a-mole game at the pizza parlor — no way to permanently win and no end in sight.

Resolving is much more satisfying and provides you freedom.

Coaching Point: *What's one thing you would you like to resolve?*

Money

CATEGORY: Quote

"Money is anything that you HAVE (meaning possess, control, have access to, can do, or can create, etc.) that you can exchange with someone else who has been persuaded that what YOU HAVE has sufficient value to exchange it for something THEY HAVE that you have been persuaded has sufficient value to make that exchange.

That is all money is or ever has been.

Many more things fit that definition than simply the currency you carry around or have in your bank account.

Money can be invented or created and expanded through powerful conversations that can be based on the past, the present or the future. It is unlimited in size and variety. It is limited only by the size and power of your imagination and your ability to engage others' imaginations in that creation."
—*John Barnes*

Coaching Point: *What would happen if you read this every day?*

SCARCITY

CATEGORY: Great Fears

To have too little, or feel you have too little, is scary for everyone. The fear of scarcity is, therefore, a major motivator in the world. Notice that (most?) advertising plays to this fear. "If you'll just buy XXXXX from us, then you can be tall/beautiful/the-envy-of-your-friends/ okay." In other words, that which you were lacking is now fixed.

If this belief that you don't have *enough* is felt and thought, then it is true for you whether evidence in the physical world supports that or not. For instance, have you ever known someone who has gone after an outcome, enjoyed getting it for milliseconds, then raised the bar to charge after even more? That behavior is usually a sign of feeling some form of scarcity.

An easy, quick, and effective way to resolve the fear of scarcity is to experience reserves. When you feel/have reserves in a given area of your life, scarcity tends to fade. Types of reserves include money, of course, but also love, health/energy/vitality, opportunities, ideas, friends/relationships, spirit, contribution, acceptance, and inspiration. You can probably add additional types of reserves to this list.

Build your reserves to eliminate the fear of scarcity. List the areas where you already have reserves and notice how different your energy is in those areas. Then pick one other area and build reserves there. Over time, the fear of scarcity fades.

Coaching Point: *What is one area in which you currently have abundant reserves and thus have no fear of scarcity?*

INVESTIGATION

CATEGORY: Quote

"There is a principle which is a bar against all information,
which is proof against all arguments
and which cannot fail to keep a man in everlasting ignorance—
that principle is — contempt prior to investigation."
—*Herbert Spencer* (and quoted by *Alcoholics Anonymous* big book)

Coaching Point: *What (about money or love or freedom or work or referrals) do you know to be absolute? Have you investigated it lately? Is it still?*

Freedom Always Has A Cost

CATEGORY: Quote

"Freedom always has a cost.

When you are in the process of earning your freedom the cost seems high.

After you have become free you realize the cost was very reasonable."

—*Steve Straus (I think it was me)*

Coaching Point: *What is your current cost for freedom?*

You Are

CATEGORY: Quote

"You are greater by far than who you are trying to become."
—*Author unknown* (perhaps it's a variation of a Patanjali quote)

Coaching Point: *You are, you really are, but people who are intent on creating a "better" future sometimes forget this. They have bought into the idea that they are somehow not enough, now, but will be, then. Not so.*

Until you learn to live the fullness of your being now, discovering who you are now, you will never become you. You are not out there. You're here. Now.

Do you already know who you are?

CREATIVITY VS. CREATIVE REPACKAGING

CATEGORY: Distinction

You spent most of the early part of your life learning about stuff by acquiring knowledge and information. You picked a profession, company or job and went about learning whatever it took to be successful. All in all, a useful process.

As you got better in your endeavors you probably found yourself taking existing information and processes and repackaging them in newly creative ways. This is a way to add value to old information and is as creative as most people get.

Real creativity is much more. When you start doing things you have not seen done before (and feel you don't have to check it out with someone first!) then you are really adding value, you are being creative. It may seem scary at first, but like a muscle that strengthens with use, you quickly start trusting yourself.

Assisting you in this process is a wealth of subtle feelings, inklings, thoughts and ideas. The more you pay attention to them, the faster will be the growth of your creativity.

Coaching Point: *Where are you already doing original work?*

LIBERTY AND SECURITY

CATEGORY: Principle

"Too many people are thinking of security instead of opportunity. They seem more afraid of life than death."
—*James F. Byrnes*

"Liberty is the right to choose. Freedom is the result of the right choice."
—*Anonymous*

"It is when we all play safe that we create a world of the utmost insecurity."
—*Dag Hammarskjold*

"Liberty means responsibility. That is why most men dread it."
—*George Bernard Shaw*

"They that can give up essential liberty to obtain a little temporary safety deserve neither liberty nor safety."
—*Benjamin Franklin*

Coaching Point: *Which do you focus on, your Liberty or your Security?*

FREE

CATEGORY: Quote

"We must be free not because we claim freedom, but because we practice it."
—*William Faulkner*

Coaching Point: *We tend to think of freedom at a nation-state level, but this is about you, about each of us.*

Where are you not free to live your life and what needs to change for you to be truly free?

In The Process vs. Attached To The Outcome

CATEGORY: Distinction

Imagine facing the task of cleaning out the over-stuffed basement of your house. You may find that the thought of what it will take to complete the job is so overwhelming you never start. Attachment to the outcome — completely cleaning it out — causes you to not begin.

When the achieving of an outcome becomes too important, you may form an attachment to it. Get the outcome and you feel good; don't get it and you feel bad. That attachment causes you to give up some of your freedom.

Another way to achieve outcomes is to just be in the process. When you have a process which you feel will achieve the outcome and then focus on getting your sense of satisfaction from simply being in action, you can win all along the way. And that's a key — get your win from being in the process, not only from accomplishing the outcome.

The process of enjoying taking one thing out of the basement each day (a daily win) will lead to the ultimate win of the cleaned-out basement.

Coaching Point: *What's something big you want to accomplish and what process can you use to achieve it?*

FLOW

CATEGORY: Principle

Everything in life is energy and information, moving from wherever it is now to wherever it's going to be next. In other words, everything is in a state of flow. You may notice this flow or not, but noticing it is useful because problems occur when you try to go against the flow.

Money, Love, Health, Relationships, Consciousness itself—each have their aspects of flow. Life gets better when you go with it. The old joke line is that it's a lot easier to direct traffic in the direction it's already going.

So why do people resist this? Attachment to outcomes; trying to get their needs met; fear, uncertainty, and doubt; lack of awareness. The reasons for resistance are many. The results of resistance are predictable.

Does this mean you should never put forth effort? No, it means if you find yourself efforting, first look to see if there is a flow in opposition. Then look to see if there is a different flow you can tap into which will give you what you want.

Flow, is. Struggle, is optional.

Coaching Point: *Where are you going with the flow right now?*

Doing Well

CATEGORY: Great Questions

"What do people who do well, do early?"

Coaching Point: *As you look around it's pretty clear that some people do really well with their lives. They have financial success, of course, but highly successful people have the rest of it also — freedom, passion, contribution, groundedness, health, relationships, whatever they consider success.*

If you were to interview them about "secrets" to their success, you would hear many of them say that they move quickly when opportunities present themselves or when something needs to be handled. Do you?

FREEDOM-TO VS. FREEDOM-FROM

CATEGORY: Distinction

When talking about having freedom, most people describe what they want freedom *from* — financial worry, unsatisfying work, a broken relationship, or some other unpleasant situation. Freedom-*from* is, at its core, a driving energy. And it works. By focusing on getting away from something, you can be powerfully motivated into action.

Freedom-*to* is a different matter. Its essence is choice. When you have filled your unmet needs, created abundant reserves, and have clarity about what brings you satisfaction and joy, you are able to focus your energy on freedom-to issues. You are free to create, develop and express.

You might decide that living in freedom-to is preferable to freedomfrom. It may be. Just don't confuse them. They are fundamentally different sources of energy.

Coaching Point: *Freedom to create your "art," whatever your art is, feels pretty good, doesn't it?*

Making A Difference

CATEGORY: Quote

"If you are not making much of a living,
chances are, you are not making much of a difference, either."
—*Mark LeBlanc (Professional Speaker)*

Coaching Point: *This quote is kind of "in your face" and it certainly doesn't apply for teachers and others who have chosen low-paying careers and yet are making a huge difference.*

But some people seem to think that making a good living will somehow "spoil" their making a difference. You can be financially successful and also be a good steward of your wealth to enhance your ability to make a difference. Mother Teresa generated millions in income and donations to further her cause.

Are you making sure you are not using a need to make a difference as an excuse to ignore earning a good living?

There Is No Should In Giving

CATEGORY: Principle

"Give until it hurts" was the fundraising slogan used by a charity several years ago. The wording was apparently intended to cause people to want to give money to their cause. It was not a highly successful campaign.

Many people seem to think that giving can be stimulated by guilt, shame, obligation, and should, as in "you should give back because you have received so much, etc."

However, there is no "should" in giving. If a should is present, something else is going on. Either you're "paying back" or "paying forward" or trying to feel good or "balancing the scales" or…

Giving is about "want-to" not should. Giving is only giving when it is unconditional, when you have no need for anything to come back to you. Giving is about feeling joy, not about becoming pain free.

Surprisingly, being unattached to getting anything back ends up returning more to you than you can ever receive and in ways you never imagined.

Coaching Point: *What is your first thought when someone mentions giving? Noticing how you react will show you something important about how you see your place in the universe. Do you want to give?*

ABUNDANCE

CATEGORY: Principle

Much has been written and said about the word *abundance*. Most of it is not too useful. When you cut through the noise, abundance is really quite simple.

Abundance is a feeling. When you have it, when you get it, when you unconsciously come from that state of being, you feel really good.

Should you make abundance one of your goals? In my experience, not really. It seems much better to have it be a by-product of living a great life. If you focus on *making* abundance happen, it's easy to get attached to some rigid metric and miss the whole point.

Notice how you feel in some area of your life where you already experience abundance. Now, imagine having that feeling spread to all areas. It's not the things, events, relationships, or metrics.

Abundance is like a deep satisfying breath. Unbounded, free.

En route to abundance you may pass through scarcity, shortage, not enough, enough, more, even much. But each of those lack the deep abiding peaceful expansion which is the state of abundance. I would argue that it is your natural state, perhaps patiently waiting for you to reclaim it.

Coaching Point: *Where do you experience abundance now?*

S:0906   WEALTH   FREEDOM

It Never Hurts To Ask

CATEGORY: Principle

Is there something you want to ask for, but find yourself holding back? Everybody holds back from asking for what they want from time to time. Why? It's just an ask. Asking doesn't seem to be that difficult. Well, it is.

If there is something you want and you're not asking for it, it's because you have one or more inner barriers in place. You're afraid: of not being able to word your ask well enough; of being thought less of for asking; of fearing having your ask rejected; of (okay, I have to do this) falling on your ask.

They're all just stories you've made up. Still, you don't ask for what you want. Because they're painful. When you touch the stories they hurt.

Solution: get clear about each inner barrier (story) and use whatever processes available to you to resolve it completely. I use a half a dozen different techniques with folks. There are countless techniques and processes around. Use them.

Until — it never hurts to ask.

Coaching Point: *What do you want to ask for now?*

Index

MONEY

S:0831 — Adding Value vs. Cutting Costs 41
S:0288 — Admire vs. Envy 44
S:0682 — Allow-Receive-Have 12
S:0458 — Business—Good vs. No vs. Bad 50
S:0751 — Checkbooks 45
S:0125 — Contentment vs. Happiness 31
S:0649 — Emotions 15
S:0012 — Financial Success is a Requirement, Not a Nicety 54
S:0753 — Flow 70
S:0297 — Freedom Always Has A Cost 64
S:0599 — Important vs. Personal 49
S:0615 — In The Process vs. Attached To The Outcome 69
S:0257 — Integrity 58
S:0902 — Luxurious vs. Luxury 34
S:0226 — Making A Difference 73
S:0652 — Money 61
S:0419 — More and Less 46
S:0690 — Real Goal vs. Tool Goal 14
S:0864 — Scarcity 62
S:0425 — Self-reliant vs. Responsible 29
S:0085 — Self-Worth 11
S:0217 — Spending Money To Get Approval 36
S:0554 — There Is No Should In Giving 74
S:0204 — Tolerance vs. Toleration 56
S:0511 — Tolerating Struggle 38
S:0155 — Value 9
S:0399 — Wealthy vs. Materialistic 47
S:0626 — What Needs To Get Funded? vs. What Do I Need To Pay For?. . .53
S:0538 — What's Next? vs. Retirement 57
S:0526 — Your Sources of Energy 25

WEALTH

S:0906 — Abundance 75
S:0288 — Admire vs. Envy.. 44
S:0877 — Adult? 20
S:0682 — Allow-Receive-Have 12
S:0225 — Attachment..55
S:0458 — Business—Good vs. No vs. Bad 50
S:0396 — Choice vs. Sacrifice... 42
S:0125 — Contentment vs. Happiness 31
S:0703 — Doing Well 71
S:0649 — Emotions...15
S:0012 — Financial Success is a Requirement, Not a Nicety......................... 54
S:0753 — Flow.. 70
S:0015 — Flow vs. Hold 48
S:0372 — Freedom-To vs. Freedom-From 72
S:0599 — Important vs. Personal 49
S:0257 — Integrity 58
S:0598 — It Is What It Is 27
S:0201 — Joy vs. Relief.. 40
S:0891 — Life Purpose 24
S:0902 — Luxurious vs. Luxury 34
S:0226 — Making A Difference 73
S:0899 — Opportunity 10
S:0212 — Quick Response 28
S:0661 — Resolve vs. Fix 60
S:0612 — Self-Awareness 19
S:0425 — Self-reliant vs. Responsible...29
S:0624 — To Not Know 21
S:0399 — Wealthy vs. Materialistic...47
S:0895 — You Are 65
S:0526 — Your Sources of Energy 25

FREEDOM

S:0437 — A New Resolution on New Year's Resolutions 43
S:0906 — Abundance 75
S:0288 — Admire vs. Envy.. 44
S:0877 — Adult? 20
S:0225 — Attachment..55
S:0728 — Be Aware vs. Beware 26
S:0833 — Being Found Out 52
S:0458 — Business—Good vs. No vs. Bad 50
S:0396 — Choice vs. Sacrifice... 42
S:0170 — Creativity vs. Creative Repackaging..66
S:0894 — Desire vs. Need..39
S:0703 — Doing Well 71
S:0649 — Emotions...15
S:0837 — Escape Key 32
S:0012 — Financial Success is a Requirement, Not a Nicety....................... 54
S:0753 — Flow.. 70
S:0015 — Flow vs. Hold 48
S:0667 — Free...68
S:0297 — Freedom Always Has A Cost 64
S:0464 — Free From Self Pre-occupation 17
S:0134 — Freedom..35
S:0393 — Freedom Provides Security..18
S:0503 — Freedom to be a Human 30
S:0372 — Freedom-To vs. Freedom-From 72
S:0195 — Freedom vs. Liberty.. 13
S:0392 — Freedom vs. Security 37
S:0257 — Integrity 58
S:0598 — It Is What It Is 27
S:0910 — It Never Hurts to Ask 76
S:0842 — Joy of Death... 51
S:0201 — Joy vs. Relief.. 40
S:0517 — Liberty and Security 67
S:0891 — Life Purpose 24
S:0898 — Obstacles.. 33
S:0212 — Quick Response..28
S:0661 — Resolve vs. Fix 60
S:0612 — Self-Awareness...19
S:0798 — Self-Deception.. 23
S:0425 — Self-reliant vs. Responsible..29
S:0143 — Several Views of Freedom 59
S:0302 — The Need To Be Self-Regulating 16
S:0554 — There Is No Should In Giving..74
S:0624 — To Not Know 21
S:0006 — Under-promise vs. Overpromise 22
S:0155 — Value 9
S:0895 — You Are 65

PURPOSE

S:0437 — A New Resolution on New Year's Resolutions 43
S:0831 — Adding Value vs. Cutting Costs...41
S:0288 — Admire vs. Envy... 44
S:0225 — Attachment.. 55
S:0751 — Checkbooks.. 45
S:0125 — Contentment vs. Happiness 31
S:0170 — Creativity vs. Creative Repackaging...................................66
S:0837 — Escape Key 32
S:0753 — Flow.. 70
S:0842 — Joy of Death.. 51
S:0201 — Joy vs. Relief.. 40
S 0891 — Life Purpose...24
S:0425 — Self-reliant vs. Responsible...29
S:0085 — Self-Worth 11
S:0554 — There Is No Should In Giving 74
S:0204 — Tolerance vs. Toleration... 56
S:0538 — What's Next? vs. Retirement 57
S:0526 — Your Sources of Energy 25

AWARENESS

S:0728 — Be Aware vs. Beware 26
S:0833 — Being Found Out.. 52
S:0458 — Business—Good vs. No vs. Bad...50
S:0894 — Desire vs. Need...39
S:0649 — Emotions... 15
S:0753 — Flow... 70
S:0464 — Free From Self Pre-occupation 17
S:0197 — Investigation 63
S:0598 — It Is What It Is 27
S:0419 — More and Less 46
S:0612 — Self-Awareness 19
S:0798 — Self-Deception... 23
S:0425 — Self-reliant vs. Responsible..29
S:0302 — The Need To Be Self-Regulating 16
S:0624 — To Not Know 21
S:0204 — Tolerance vs. Toleration.. 56
S:0006 — Under-promise vs. Overpromise... 22

Facilitator's Guide

FOR FAMILIES: I know of families who have weekly meetings to discuss whatever is on the family members' minds — to communicate, make requests, clear the air, etc. — and who start each meeting by having someone read a "Steve's 3-Minute Coaching" which is of particular interest to them. The group will then discuss it for a few minutes, learning and growing in the process. It is a healthy way to set the tone for the rest of the meeting. I must tell you, I was deeply moved when I first heard about this use of my weekly offerings. Assisting people to communicate and connect is core to my life purpose.

FOR BUSINESSES: Others will start a business meeting by reading an S3MC which is germane to their meeting. Picture a sales meeting, or a planning meeting, or a product redesign meeting, or a whatever meeting, starting off with a breath of thought from the "outside." It sets a nice tone.

FOR OTHER GROUPS: Some service clubs (such as Rotary, etc.) have

started their meetings with an S3MC to get everyone on the same page and stimulate thought and engagement. Also Toastmasters and other professional and trade groups use them as meeting kick-starters.

If you choose to use the contents of this book for a group you're part of, in the next section I have some suggested questions which might stimulate your group's thought.

Facilitator Questions

The following questions are in addition to the one which forms the "Coaching Point" at the end of each entry in the book. Start with the Coaching Point question, then use the appropriate ones below.

- What about this appeals/resonates with you most?
- What part of this do you disagree with?
- What is an example of this you've seen?
- Is this about data, information, knowledge, or wisdom?
- How will this change what we/you do now?
- If we/you implement this, what will be lost?
- What about this is easy?
- What about this is hard?
- What is the first step to implementing this?
- What is the small first step of that first step?
- Who will be most impacted by this?
- Who will benefit most by this?

ACKNOWLEDGMENTS

This book has come into being because of Barbara Dee. I had never known what the real role of an editor was in the production of a book. I do now. Sure, the source material for this book was already created over an eighteen-year period through the weekly publication of the *Steve's 3-Minute Coaching* (S3MC) email and blog. And, sure, I've known for some time that I wanted to create books which were extractions of that material. Even many readers, friends, and colleagues have told me to do so. But not until Barbara came on board to edit the project did it happen. She has been a tireless co-creator, a constant inspiration, a knowledgeable publishing resource, and, yes, an occasional kick-in-the-pants to keep me on point. Most of the "Acknowledgments" pages I've read in other books give a shout-out to the editor, usually toward the end, and sometimes it comes across as merely an obligation by the author. Not this time. Barbara, thank you, we got this done together!

Speaking of co-creators, every single issue of the weekly S3MC, once written, passed under the discerning eye of my wife, Pam. You readers will never know how much I wrote which got a nose-crinkle from her, resulting in either a rewrite or a short trip to the shredder. As a lifetime reader of good writing, Pam's opinion has been my gold standard for what I release. Thank you, dear.

Speaking of thank-you's, the subscribers to the S3MC have given me ideas and feedback for every issue I've released. While I've tried to acknowledge each one individually, let me here thank you collectively. We are a community of likeminded folks interested in learning, growing, and having an expanded view of life. Keep your comments coming.

Finally, I thank the many Coaches, guides, mentors, teachers, and fellow travelers who have inspired me and encouraged me to step out and say what I'm here to say. It would have been easy for me to hold back, remaining safely in the shadows, keeping my thoughts and observations to myself. You folks wouldn't let me do that. Just as I encourage people to "live the full expression of your life" so, too, you help make sure I do the same. Onward!

Steve Straus—The Coach, June 2013

About The Author

Today the idea of having a Coach, or even being a Coach, is well understood, but back in January of 1987 there was no (general) coaching profession. The response from most people, upon hearing that Steve Straus was a Coach, was to ask, "What sport?" A reasonable question given that the role of a sports coach is to assist athletes to be their best, to set goals, to excel, whatever their game. That's what personal Coaches do for people in the game of life.

As Steve learned and grew in the emerging and evolving profession of Coaching — labeled variously Life/Executive/Success/Business Coach, or some other modifier — he discovered he enjoyed finding or creating useful little chunks of information and wisdom and sharing them with people who were interested in learning, growing, and having a great life. Thus was born, in August of 1995, what became known as *Steve's 3-Minute Coaching*, a weekly email/blog with readers around the world. These principles, distinctions, and gems of wisdom are the source of the contents of this book.

But a question remains, who is Steve Straus? What is his background, and more importantly, what has positioned him to provide guidance and support for people on their journey through life? The short answer is this is what he's here to do, to be. This is the expression of his purpose in life. You might not think so given his formal education in Mechanical Engineering and Finance, or his early career in computer technology. Yes, he was a nerd! But a nerd who continued to be drawn to the people side of the tech world rather than the bits and bytes of the boxes.

From teaching technology (he said standing in front of a room full of people was as scary as anything he had done to-date) to system support for users, to sales, to starting his own businesses, he found increasing interest in the human experience, and the journey of life.

Fast forward to becoming a professional speaker, designing and delivering public workshops, writing and publishing an early eBook, and then the greatest traction — assisting in the development of a Coach training curriculum, teaching and encouraging the new communication technology of Coaching.

Through his entire career Steve Straus has been interested in discovering why some people seem to lead successful, satisfying lives while others don't. He is continually in the question of, "What's the difference that makes the difference?"

Steve's clients, webinar students, and now readers around the world can benefit from his quest for useful, practical wisdom, published in the series *A Little Book of Working Wisdom*.

Steve's other pursuits take him into the countryside of southeast Arkansas where he and his wife Pam have a working timber farm. They live most of the time on a bluff overlooking a large lake north of Dallas, Texas. One of his joys is that his business model makes him geographically independent — wherever there is a phone and an internet connection, he's in business.

In addition to writing several more books, Steve plans to expand his general aviation flying, discover the wily habits of largemouth bass, and take long, unstructured driving trips to discover what's over the next hill.

Learn more about Steve Straus, The Coach, by visiting these three web sites:

This web site contains all the archives, books, and other products related to *Steve's 3-Minute Coaching* blog.

Steves3MinuteCoaching.com

This site has all the information about private and group coaching. Steve has coached business owners, executives, professionals, entrepreneurs, high-net-worth individuals, people transitioning to retirement, and master coaches, since 1987.

StrausUSA.com

This web site offers a wide range of leading-edge training programs in both live and recorded formats: efficient, modern, topic-specific training you need.

VirtualTrainingU.com

Money, Wealth & Freedom:
A Little Book Of Working Wisdom

TO ORDER additional print copies of
Money, Wealth & Freedom
please visit:

www.Steves3MinuteCoaching.com

Discounts for Volume Orders:
Group facilitation, business meeting leaders,
client and corporate gifts, family gifts,
leadership training and human resource managers
-Please visit:
www.Steves3MinuteCoaching.com

E-Book versions of this book are available for Kindle
and most e-reading devices.
For a direct link, please visit:
www.Steves3MinuteCoaching.com